ROBERT FERGUSON

EVERYONE ON MY STREET

novum ◢ pro

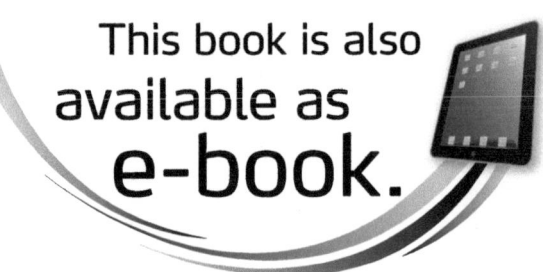

www.novum-publishing.co.uk

© 2024 novum publishing

ISBN 978-3-99146-490-7
Editing: Stephanie Marrie
Cover photo:
Natali Dobrovolskaya | Dreamstime.com
Cover design, layout & typesetting:
novum publishing

www.novum-publishing.co.uk

Climate neutral
Print product
ClimatePartner.com/16547-2201-1002

CONTENTS

ACKNOWLEDGEMENTS

The following poems were first published
in Novum #13, vol. 5:
"Trans*", *"Visitation"*, *"Namaste"* and
"Where have you been, love?"
Most of the others grow from the inspirations
provided by Lydia Towsey and particularly Charlie Jordan,
muse beyond compare.

INTRODUCTION

Of the total UK population, more than half live in major towns according to the 2021 census, and only a tenth in rural areas. This explains why the streets in our towns and cities are crowded and buzz, while a country walk is likely to be quiet and lonely – except for the cars rushing from one town to another down rat-run country roads.

Not only are our urban streets becoming busier, the people in them are becoming ever more fascinatingly varied. In 2021, apparently, similar proportions of the UK population were of people aged under fifteen and over sixty-five (about a fifth each), or of a different skin colour, culture or dress code from pale grey and British-pink. Also, a slightly greater proportion was in some way disabled (a quarter, and remember, you can't always see the symptoms of a person's disability as you walk past them), and at least 1.7 million people in England and Wales (2.8% of the population) claimed a gender other than that attributed to them at birth.

This collection of poems tries to stand with the people of the minorities in our society. It tries to draw on their richness and revel in their gifts to the rest of us; and sometimes just reminds the majority that difference so often offers us opportunities which we will be the poorer for overlooking.

Robert Ferguson
Summer 2023

INAPPROPRIATE?

I'd valued you so much and for so long,
Wished I dared offer a hug, but did so fear
It's newness would frighten you.

If I were to try, would it change our relationship?
Would you feel unable to come back again
And give me what I so much appreciate each day?

Just once, without thinking, in a conversation,
I stretched out my arms in sympathy
And you came to me, gladly and giggling with thanks.

Next visit, you were just the same as always,
Beautiful and kind and gentle, quick and strong.
I had to be the same, and so I was.

HER CHOICE, NOT MINE

We tried to relate
My sister suggested him
But he was a void

    She thought I needed
    A man in a lonely life
    Between hairdressers

        I didn't. So what?
        He seemed well dressed, clean shaven
        She could take him home

            But her husband Al
            Wouldn't understand, of course
            Though they are both bored

        So, working with him,
        Trusting and attracted, she
        Must pass him on

Why me? That's trust too
Pity it didn't work for us
He bored me, just like Al

LOST

Lawn, leaf-surrounded, bailey round the house
Beyond which is my shed-motte sanctuary
Where pen and cushion wait to welcome me
Back from the bustling world, back to a peace
I am precluded from by thunderstorms
And traffic crashing past my open gate.
Deep in the flowerbed weeds your bracelet lies
Tarnished no doubt, now dull and lost for ever
In fact, but never from my memory.

WHERE HAVE YOU BEEN, LOVE?

Where have you been, love? I haven't felt you in years,
Your tremoring indecision about everything,
Clothes, colours, lens or glasses,
Tea or coffee, bus or cab or walk?
What would she like or hate,
Put up with or accidentally match in taste?
What present would she like, one for herself
Or for her home? When is her birthday?
Is her sign compatible with mine?
Or opposite? If so, is that why I'm attracted?
Where have you been, love? Never seen a girl
Like this, in the office, in the street? Or just asleep
For all this time, and only now awake?

How are you, heart? You'll see her in an hour
In a new dress and earrings you haven't seen before.
She'll smile as you pull back her restaurant chair,
Knowing what you're doing, slipping into her seat,
Putting her purse on the table, no mobile in sight.
How are you, heart, as you contemplate all this,
Not knowing her well yet, but hoping that her heart
Will be equally as excited as you are.

POIGNANT

Before We Opened

> Why am I stuck here
> Alone until opening?
> Where are you, Johnny?

Café Breakfast

> Only just opened
> Coffee machine spits and drips
> Will he come today?

DANGEROUS DIVING

I've never done it, stood on the edge of a cliff
A hundred feet above the sea, with the intention
Of diving out and down so gracefully
To enter the water below with ne'er a splash.
I'm doing it this evening without a cliff,
Or sea below. I'm meeting my new therapist for the first time
And throwing my self, my fears, my life into her hands.

Who will she be? I mean, I know her name,
At least the name she's given me to use,
But who is she? Google offers many therapists with her name.
Which one is she? Is it a generic name they take
To hide their true selves confidentially?
"This session is just to get to know each other
And decide if we will fit, be able to work together,"
She said on the telephone,
But does she really mean, for her to judge
If why I sought her out is just too shocking
For her to face? Logic suggests she's heard it all before.
My shame and fear suggest the opposite,
But I am not so very special.

A young woman, she sounded,
Like my granddaughter,
But, if she is that age, will she appreciate the world
In which I grew and formed and hurt and bent
To shapes that now I wish I had resisted?

What will she ask? What will I have the courage
To tell her truthfully? And yet, if I shirk this,
Whatever will be the point of gathering up my strength
To seek her help? *Who am I?* she might ask.
I cannot say. *What moves my soul?* Nor that.
This is far worse than interviewing for a job,
But unavoidable now, for here I am.

DAVID

There he was, standing in front of me
When I hadn't seen him in years,
And, when I last saw him, we fought
Like cat and dog. Literally! He accused me
Of almost breaking his jaw.
It was a beautiful punch.
He couldn't have forgotten it,
But here he was now, an expert when I needed one.
"These are great cameras. Easy extra lens attachment.
Simple, no-trouble insurance." I chose and paid
As much an old friend as a client.

He died six months later of leukaemia
At the age of twenty-three, while I was still abroad.
Was it a magical meeting?

        "I forgive you, and goodbye."

ESCAPER

He sat at the back of the class, behind bigger students,
And just simply drifted off, escaped,
Eyes half-closed, head still facing forward,
But empty and glazed, just not there.

We didn't know where he'd gone to, or when.
But we formed his escape committee
And every time a teacher began
To ask him a question, hands would sprout up
All over the room.

"Sir, Sir," piping voices would pierce the air,
And distracting questions would be insisted.
"Sir, if it doesn't stop raining soon,
Will this afternoon's games be cancelled?"
And, "Sir, what's that woman doing there by the bus stop?"
And he would get clean away.

He always came back in plenty of time
To go home, and he never said
Where he'd been or when he'd got back
Or who he'd seen anywhere on his way,
But he didn't miss much, came top every time
We were tested, and no-one let on.

I didn't hear what happened to him later.
Maybe it's best not to ask,
But once an inveterate escaper gets a taste for it,
There's no knowing when he'll leave you
Or if or when he'll return.

KINDLY MR. GRUMP

If I had the power I crave
To influence those around me
I would give to everyone
The gift of organisation.
No-one would ever miss a bus
Or burn the toast,
Come late to dates or meetings,
Forget their 'phones, misplace their keys
Or inconvenience their friends
By overstaying welcomes.

WHO MAKES IT A HOME?

He never comes into the house, but I can't lift or bend.
My sister-in-law passed him on to me
When it all became too much for her, and she went into care.
I take him his tea on a tray
With his pay tucked under his biscuit-plate.
When it's wet, I put it in the greenhouse,
When dry, on the garden bench
Beneath the apple trees at the end of the lawn,
And he trims and clips and tidies
And makes the whole place home.

BY THE POND

The geese quack and flap down from the farmyard
All eighteen of them, so self-important,
Like the members of a country fête committee
A week before The Date with nothing done.
The red tiles on the milking parlour roof
Melt in the sun and warm the yellow cat
Who lies across them dozing, like an emperor
Displayed to the world in his power and elegance,
Only the tip of his tail flipping gently
To left, to right,
And I siesta in the long grass beside the pond.

OBSERVATION

Directly opposite the garden gate –
Adore them, praise them, grasp them in your heart,
The while assessing colour, movement, grace –
Three things apparent
A bush, a bloom, a butterfly
Grouped close together, totally dependent.
Instructive love binds them, keeps them with each other,
Feeds them, strengthens and defends them,
If only for a tiny speck of time.

SECURITY ON WHEELS

(Granada, Spain)

He zips across the *plaza*, eyes everywhere,
On the pools of tourists, the leather workers' bags
Displayed on blankets, late breakfasters
Feeling the growing heat, escaping the office
For a quick or not-so-quick *espresso*.
He knows them all, by action if not name
And sees no trouble here, so swings his hips,
Changes direction and leans into the corner,
Patrols the shady *avenida's* pavement, past the banks
And lawyers' offices, dentists' and the green cross pharmacy.
A friend hails, offers coffee, he leans forward and his wheels
Stop turning but he stands above the heads
And tables to swallow the contents of the tiny cup
Handed up from a passing waiter's elevated tray.
Then off again, speed, balance co-ordinated
Dancing through the dominated, parting crowd.

MY MATE ...

"Haven't you anything else to spread on my toast?"
I asked, so she demonstrated her love
By rising and fetching a yoghurt from the 'fridge
And stirring the Marmite into the yoghurt pot.
"What a waste of yoghurt!" I exploded
So she rose again and walked to the corner cupboard,
Returning with peanut butter and a banana.
"No, no," I said, "I have a peanut allergy
And the banana will be soft and brown inside."
"Did you enjoy this evening's curry?" she asked me.
"What do you think I spiced it with?" She smiled.

SILENCE

It was huge. Darkness almost hid the painted ceiling.
It was square. The floor was covered with chairs.
At first it seemed that nobody else was there
Until my eyes adjusted to the gloom
And a figure far from the narrow door unfolded
Only slightly, silently, offered neither welcome nor
interruption,
Looked to where an altar glowed, and bent again.
The world seemed to have emptied of everything,
Nature, manufacture, life itself, the ability to breathe.
Just Spirit, hovering weightless in the space.

SUBVERSION

Why didn't they tell us where we'd come to live?
They planned the road outside, and blocked it off
As a cul-de-sac, a crescent,
Planted trees as if to make an avenue
But everybody parks here, dropping off
The kids for school, Grandma for the doctor or chiropodist.
They put up street lamps, telephone wires on poles,
Even allowed the cable TV company to dig holes
And sink trenches in their brand new pavements
But they didn't give our home a place, a name.
So we did.
Evelyn called a meeting at her house,
Invited everyone, and almost everybody came.
Beer, wine and crackers, and lots and lots of chat.
We bought a metal plate, and bright white paint,
Dug our own hole and put our sign in place
And there it stands. But, no,
I will not tell you where we live, my friend.
You must just come and find us for yourself.
The Council can't

IF I COULD KEEP A SHOP

If I could keep a shop
I would stock biscuits in tin boxes
Which everyone could see through the glass window
In the lid, and ribbons so the girls would visit me
To dress their hair, and umbrellas and bicycle pumps
For the unwary taken by surprise by a disaster,
And coffee, tea and sugar for those who run out,
And the odd ball of wool for peoples' new kittens,
And ... everything that neighbours need,
So that I would never be lonely again.

THE LONGHOUSE

One small room wide, whitewashed of course,
To stand out against the hawthorn hedges and bare soil
Where the vegetables grew, when the sun released them
From the shadow of the scree-stippled mountain
With its cwm-lake and ice-carved sides.
Black and white cows spotted the dark green grass and yellow
gorse,
Grey shaggy sheep between them
Nipping their lambs to teach them discipline.
And Auntie loved them, healed their barbed-wire scratches,
Hand-milked them all, churned butter, swept curds off whey
And made cheese and yoghurt as she always had.
She lived in the Western end of the house,
They to the East, their warmth extending to her blanketed bed,
Their smell comforting her, and their occasional stirrings
In the hay she'd spread for them.
What would they do when she'd gone? Where would they go?
Who would repair the thatch, thick as her soda bread
Preserving the seaweed brought from the beach below?
For the house would continue without her, she knew that
And grunted stiffly as she returned to sleep.

FORMERLY

I have not always lived here.
Once, I had a caravan and faithful horse
With blinkers and a nosebag, and a way
Of stamping his great hooves to make the sparks fly
From his shining shoes.

Sometimes a farmer let us bath in his rain-butt,
Sometimes gave us tea or soup from his kitchen door,
Eggs or a rasher of his home-cured bacon,
And sometimes we just plodded on the road
To somewhere else. But now I'm here.

The caravan has gone to a museum.
The knacker took the horse, so now he's glue,
Still serving useful purpose as he did for me
When we clip-clopped together for no purpose
But our pleasure,

> Which is how I live now,
> As I used to live before.

AROMATHERAPY

As the flame burns my finger, and
My nose twitches, a gentle cough
Claws its way out of my throat
And I see the exotic throne-room
Of an ancient king, to which rich
Gold and scarlet blossoms have been brought
To smoulder for his pleasure at his feet.

INCLUSIVE SOUP

I waded down the pavement past a mixture of street traders
Seeing colours in bright splashes
Hearing calls and gentler voices
Talking, singing, shouting, cooing,
In languages from truly everywhere
With unfamiliar words and gestures
Unfamiliar smells and shapes in the crates of vegetables
Hugs for love and slack embraces say hello, goodbye and see you
Standing, sitting, striding, looking,
Stirred together, gently heated
By their freedom, by their journeys,
By the hope and comfort travellers find
Now feeling safe in their community
Settled, seeped well in their neighbours
In a welcoming society
Soft as cream and sweet as barley
Arms and lives stretched out to love.

BLACK

Black as coal.
Black as a cat.
        But you're not black,
        Just a handsome brown
        Like long, strong tropical wood
        Matured, hardened in the world
        Given an honourable purpose by the skills and love
        Of hands and teachers, with a brain, a saw,
        A rasp and sandpaper, polish, oil and wax.
        Joints to hold forever,
            Drawers to slide
                Silken, like the smoothness of your skin.

Black is unavoidable in the white world your parents came to,
That in which they brought you up, protected and comforted
you
When the bullies struck. It will take time,
But gradually black is coming good,
Influencing attitudes as black appears
In music, poetry, architecture,
Parliament, contributing, participating, leading,
Taking a top place as us in us
To be unnoticed and unquestioned soon.

SNOW HAIKUS

Heavy cloud above us
Snow will fall soon from the sky
Your smile is hidden

                    Where did we come from?
                    Somewhere caring or careless,
                    Sunny or snowy?

DISABLED BALLET

It might have cost a lot of time
Organising taxis, confirming where to eat,
Ensuring accessible toilets were available
BEFORE booking tables and seats,
But it was worth it to see her face.
Her first ever ballet, first theatre for years,
Her first real sparkle since we met
Months and months ago.
Wonderful meal, wonderful ice creams
And interval drinks, and excellent seats
With the best view of all in the theatre.
"It was like magic!" she said.

BEST INTENTIONS

I cut a corner, and really shouldn't have done.
The shops were shut and I was too impatient.
I worried I wouldn't have bought your favourite chocolates
Before we got to the theatre, so I ordered them on line
And they arrived squashed and melted into one another.
Wherever had they been?
So I did the only possible, sensible thing.
I ate them, and took you a beautiful scarf instead.

HOW TO SLOW DOWN

Rushing is a habit, and sometimes it helps
But it probably means you've taken on too much.
Say no!
Choose what *you* want to do.
Resist other people's expectations.
They are *theirs*, not always yours.
They carry responsibilities which they are seeking to transfer
To *you*, or anybody else they can.
It's likely their respect will be enhanced
By your refusal.
You are strong!

I AM A TORTOISE

The tortoise extends his head
And then his tail, cautiously,
Though he knows where he is.
It isn't far from where he stopped before
And retracted his head and tail and legs while he waited
To be sure of his security.
He didn't reach his present age without being careful.
He reaches out a leg, and then another one,
Pauses to rebalance his shell and look around.
Nothing here to eat.
Moves on through damp grass
Towards the lettuce patch, in hope.

ALTERNATIVES

If I'd left school at eighteen, and not gone to university
As most people didn't in those days,
If I'd done National Service in a barracks
With all the other squaddies,
Learned to smoke, and do guard duty on cold days,
If, like my friend, I'd become a solicitor in a provincial town,
And thought a holiday in Wales was foreign,
I wouldn't have met you.
Our daughter wouldn't exist,
Or our grandsons.
Would the world have been better?
Who would I be now, or anybody else
I might have met somewhere along the line?

WINTER HIDING

I hide
From winter's wet
And cold and fog and dark
Early in the evening, and
Keep warm

Beside
The crackling fire
Till bedtime, when, undressed,
I hide with wool socks, hot bottle,
And sleep

DRIVEN AWAY

They close the door behind them,
Feel the tension dissipate.
"Your mother! Getting worse," he says.
"No, just the same, but we'd forgotten,
Having been away so long."
"I like America," he says,
"But sad we have to go so far."
"No problem, is it? She will soon be dead."

PEACE IN COMMUNITY
(for Lucy)

Everything's quiet about five o'clock.
The café's empty, the cleaners have gone home,
Everyone else is cooking their tea.
Carers are busy checking the vulnerable,
Attending to dressings, blood pressures, pills,
And, at long last, there's a pause in the chatter
In communal areas. It's otherwise deafening,
But now there's a silence, and here I sit
Not even pretending to read, just sitting,
Eyes closed, in my wheelchair, in total peace.

FEAR AND LOVE

I frightened my carer this morning
I was asleep when she came in
I think she thought I had passed away
It would have made her late, if I had,
But, no, I woke up
And the look on her face was pure love.

ONLY A PARTIAL IMPACT

New, modern, vibrant décor, and quite near.
I could get in, but couldn't get about.
The tables were too low for wheelchaired knees.
The steps precluded me from joining in
The open mic events on lower floors.
The loos were all upstairs, the arrow said.
All I could do was hold it in and hope.
So why not bring the poets up, the toilets down?
I was excluded by those who couldn't think
Of *functions* – what the place was *for*, and who
Might want – might *need* – to use it.
We, the disabled in some ways, are capable in others.
We, who cannot walk, can think and speak
And interpret the world to other people,
Teach by our words, *if only they'd let us in!*

None of us does everything as well as someone else.
I can no longer travel, but I have more time to read.
I can no longer travel, but I can communicate.
Just because my legs won't work, that doesn't yet affect my head.
I can still offer contributions others sometimes need.

Just give me time, five times, to dress,
Or reload paper in the printer,
Put away delivered shopping,
Pick up something from the floor.
Give me equal time with others for the things I still can do.
I am only partially impacted by my impairment.
Everything else is working perfectly.

PEDESTRIAN – BUT I'M NOT

They built a lovely pedestrian precinct
In our town, and all the popular shops
Flocked there.
No traffic, no hooting, no fumes,
No accidents to the elderly, children, 'phone users.
But bits of it they cobbled, so old people tripped,
Cut their skulls. Wheelchairs and prams only got
From one shop to another with spine-rending bumps.
Just another good idea gone wrong
For lack of recognition that we're not all the same.

HOME IN A FEW LINES

A place for everything
Nothing out of place
    Until a friend drops in
    Wanders about
    Picks things up
    Puts them down
        Elsewhere – out of reach.

SIBLING RIVALRY

My body and mind are related
But sometimes they don't communicate
As I would like them to do.
For instance, my mind says to my legs,
"Straighten!" and my legs refuse,
So I push on my gym-strengthened arms
And the pain in my thighs makes me squeak
(Euphemism!)
and my legs straighten up under protest.
I balance to button my jacket
Using both hands, and my legs revolt.
I sit down heavily, but at least
Not on the floor this time.
My brain believes it's only thirty-five,
But my legs know they're eighty
And demand respect. Between them, where am I?
Sometimes one, but many times the other.
Just never in control.

MY NECK

Snap, crackle, crunch. Not breakfast.
Just my neck, waking up from
Eight hours off the edge of the pillow
And resenting the weight of my head.

Creak, groan and scream, but I must
Move my head (that's your job, neck!)
So my eyes can see the clock
And, the other way, the dawn in the window.

An oath, from the throat where the voice
Comes up through the neck
Which still won't turn without pain,
But so much depends on you, neck.

                              Keep going.

FLASHBACK

They rolled his new wardrobe out of the van
And into the house on a platform
With a castor on each corner,

And he recalled the small boy he'd seen in Algiers
Twenty years ago, on just such a platform,
Begging at pavement cafes,

Scooting from table to table,
Pulling himself along by the legs of the furniture
Because he had no feet or legs below his knees,

No food, no home, no parents,
Nothing but a wary determination to continue
Such limited existence as remained to him.

EXCLUDED

I am not so much disabled as excluded
By the more fortunate, unthinking, unimaginative majority.
Though I can't stand, I can see, hold, think.
I'm not a messy eater. I don't drool.
But my wheelchair is too wide to go through some doors,
It won't climb steps, or turn corners in narrow corridors,
All issues forced on me by architects
Who spend their lives
Ignoring me, and hoping I'll stay quiet.
Sorry, guys.

EXHAUSTION

4.1 kilometres! Ticking through
The last few seconds. Dry mouth.
Sweat, puffing, if only for two minutes
At the end. But like
That last cross-country push
Up the ploughed hillside
Towards the out-of-focus finish
And the cheers, so many years ago.

ODE TO MY BODY

What courage, what bravery, to proceed
Despite the gun-shot shattered hips and knees
To struggle through the pain, eyes open,
Refusing sleep, refusing rest, refusing utterly to let go
Until one foot at last makes up its mind to move
Towards a chair from which I can
Eventually rise

PATIENCE

Patience has cerebral palsy.
She didn't ask for it.
She's beautiful, but wheelchair-bound
And wobbly, and her speech is indistinct and slow.
When she needs something,
People try to help by guessing.
Because her mind is sharp and funny and imaginative,
They usually get it wrong.
She tries to explain, but they won't wait.
They try again, and get it wrong again.
"Which way to ..." Patience says.
"The hospital's down there, my dear," they say.
"No, ..." "The Church is that way"
"No, ..." "The Benefit Office ...", pointing a helpful finger.
Patience sometimes runs out of patience.
Rolls off with a smile in her wheelchair.
Surely, somebody knows how to find a public loo?

WE ARE PART OF THE WORLD

Joe makes complicated electric light displays
To put in shops at Christmas,
Giving them to others to put up
Because ladders are beyond him now.

From his wheelchair, he instructs apprentices,
Giving them the benefit of experience
They could find nowhere else.
Round and round he scurries on his wheels

Laying out cables between neon tubes
Which the boys and girls will warm and bend,
Load, with him, into vans and take round the district
To distribute.

                     He misses his legs, of course,
But not as much as the world would miss
His expertise, if he were to be written off
As just another useless, broken cripple.

EATING OUT

She slammed the cup down on the table,
Just out of reach as usual.
"Cutlery by the counter," she sniffed,
And scowled as my wheelchair spins to one side
To collect a spoon where she'd hidden them
Round a corner beyond the kitchen door.
As she passes, I say, "Salt and pepper?"
Another sniff, another slam, to stand them
Two inches beyond my range again, but someone else,
An unknown neighbour, smiles and stretches
To push them across, and turns away.
Kindness survives, even when it is sometimes shy.

SAINT RUE

Whenever you're down and frustrated
Because you can't go or can't reach,
And a stranger's hand and strength stretch out
To help you, look carefully.

Did she have
Red hair in waves, and a luminous dress,
And a halo, transparent shepherd's crook,
Blue Doc Martens, a wheelchair,
And a Scottish accent?

If so, she was no stranger.
That was Saint Rue, patron of all the disabled,
Whose mission is to help in alien places
And bring us joy where we think no joy can be.

WHEN SOMEONE DIES

When someone dies, the road forks
Round the gap they leave
In the bed, at the table, through that door,
And you can bury yourself with them,
Do nothing constructive in the space they left,
Leave empty the time you took about your duties;
Or grasp the gifts offered by your freedom.
New people with new attitudes will float up
Into your life.
New skills, new occupations, will arise
You never thought of, never dared to try.
New attitudes, new tolerances stride ahead
Down one road. Down the other,
Tight fingers cling to former constancy,
Time closes round the chances left ungrasped.

OUR FAVOURITE BISCUIT

On the street leading up from the river,
Above the old Palladian bridge,
You said, "I came here for coffee years ago,
Digging my father out from his office to treat me
On Saturday morning, after I'd finished school
(Banks opened on Saturdays then),
And felt grown up at fourteen,
Sitting among the town's fashions and furs.
Let's go in." So we did, and had rich, dark coffee
And Bath Olivers on gold-edged side-plates,
Just as she used to do.
Oh, the taste and the touch of those biscuits!
The firm rich chocolate offset by the coffee,
Unsobered by the plainest biscuit
You could find anywhere!
And I haven't eaten them since – too expensive,
But we were on holiday then down memory lane,
So what the hell!

A WIDOWER'S GHOST

Why does the furniture move
Around the bedroom?
Who's is the ghost who drives
The bed away from the light switch,
Folds the blankets out of reach,
Pushes pillows sideways,
Hides tiny dropped pain-killers out of sight
Behind the bedspread hem,
Tilts pictures just so far out of true
As to irritate but not to hide?
No-one else visits these days and
I deny nudging or leaning or pushing things
Across the shiny floor.
Is this your shade, warning me
You're still here, keeping an eye
On my loyalty? No need.
My comforts these days
Come from a good book and radio,
Even though the bed is lonely and cold.

DAFFODILS

Ever since I looked in the bag and found
Brown orbs with crispy skins like onions
And popped them in the holes
Made by my dibber
Beside the garden path of my unhappy neighbour
I've hoped that, when their trumpets blast
Their welcome to the Spring
And nod cheeringly at him
Through his slammed-closed window of defence,
His heart may ease within him
At least as much as to let him say hello.

PLEASURE AND JOY

I met Diane with a big black dog.
Well, Diane had the dog, which walked by her side
Obediently, until she stopped, and the dog stopped
Too, and sat beside my wheelchair
To lick my held-out hand. Then she shifted round
(The dog) to put her tail beneath my wheelchair's tyre
So I couldn't abandon her.
I scratched her head (the dog's) and she bent it back
So I could reach it better to give her pleasure,
And thought of nothing else for quite a while.

INDIGNATION

Tired for a moment, I sat on a fallen branch
To find myself assaulted by the voice
Fortissimo of the shrill occupier of
The shelter under the hedge, behind the tree.
"I was here first," the wren was shouting,
"My mate will be back soon, and see you off,
You blaggard! You've disturbed my children,
And put them in the shade. Move on!"
What could I do? I leaned upon my stick,
Stood up and staggered on
To find another perch,
The whole of nature unified against me.

RESOLUTION

This year, I'm going to invite two pets to live with me.
One would be lonely, two can learn not to fight.
They say there are plenty at the Pets' Protection League,
All sizes, all shapes, all colours, all characters.
What I need is someone to observe.
I've analysed myself to death.
I go out very little, sit in my chair a lot
And now I need someone else to attract
My eye, my hand, my amusement, my wondering.
What does that mean? What does that say?
What do you want now? Why through that door?
They wouldn't get lonely, and would come back
If they slipped past the supermarket delivery man to explore.
They'd know who supplied their food and drink,
And a warm soft bed and company at night.

I REALLY NEED ...

I really need a pussycat
Because they're beautiful
And efficient
In their movements
In their decisions
In their likes and dislikes
Choosing between people and places and food
And presents and prey.

She (it must be) would teach me
To be graceful in my gestures
Wholehearted in my love
Relentless in my demands
Clear in the expression of my needs
Unembarrassed in any company
Doing anything, anywhere,
Whether polite or not.

VISITOR, OR ...

I don't think she knocked, but the window rattled
And an apparition waved her tail at me
Through the darkened pane.

I tried to look away but couldn't.
She had caught my eyes in hers,
Demanding access to my lonely life.

The window opened to a tiny fraction,
Her sandy paw tucked itself into the gap
Like a salesman's foot tucked under a front door.

"May I come in," it said. "Of course I may",
And in she came, carefully,
Squeezing past my hand

Sat on the window sill, elegant,
Meticulously washed a paw
And choose what she wanted to do.

I sat in the ample armchair beside the fire.
She sprang lightly, floating in air, onto my knee,
Put her claws in, curled round and round twice to make

A nest in my lap, closed her eyes, and began to give off
A deep, continuous, satisfied, long drawn out
Purrrrrrrrr.

NOT NEARLY ALL OF ME

For the present, there is only one of me,
At this meeting, at this party, on this bus,
At my mother's table after Father's death
With nothing much of weeping but, as always,
Great concern that, without income, she might drown
And I, there, man at last and needed,
Sorting the paperwork she'd never seen.

But here's another me, in Father's local
With all his friends around. "He's just got home
From London," full of pride; and so was I.
Not puffed up arrogant exactly, but well pleased.

And once again, on the back seat of the team coach,
Accepted for my size and the success of that last try,
But fearing they might guess I'd rather played
Goal defence, and looking forward to an evening spent
In bars with friends I hoped they'd never meet.

Now the Chairman, calling the meeting to order,
A busy agenda and they know that I
Am not one to waste time on conversation.
Pure pointed business me, purpose and outcome
And please give me a plan by Thursday week
To show how both may easily be achieved.

How many of us are there crammed by circumstance
Into each mind and body, brain and mouth?
How many more exist than we dare show the world?
What does our fear or conscience hedge about?

TRANS*

My dress is white with a bold red roses print
And wide straps to hold it on my bare shoulders.
Over it, a lacey black Spanish mantilla drapes unnecessarily
Round my upper arms, above a tiny crimson clutch
And bright red shoes. My skirt sways as I step outside,
Turning to close my door, and dare expose
Myself to the judgement of the world.
I am a woman, though that world once knew
Me as a short and skinny man, since that was the assignment
Given to my body when I left my mother's womb.
That was what the midwife saw, but no way
Could she see my heart, my instincts, in the place
Where gender dwells, has always dwelled, despite
The binary parcels into which the unimaginative
Allocate everyone they never know.
So here I am at last, taking the pavement
To my local shop, and dreading what they'll say.
But, oh, the joy to be myself, so much much better,
Whatever they say, than who I was before.

NAMASTE

Hands together before the eyes
Reject the fearful scene
Hands together before the mouth
Hides the shock, contains the scream
Hands together before the heart says, "Welcome
I give myself to you and to your service"

EMPTY

Empty as the surface of a pond
At sunset. Neither wind-driven ripples
Or the fins of fish disturb its stillness.

Hollow as an old oak
Which has been growing, standing, dying here
Since before the pond was dug.

Open as the fell rising above the field
Bare, changing upwards green to brown to grey
From grass to heather, scree to shining rock.

Threatening as a crevasse, darkening deeper
Into the green-blue ice, its edges sculpted
By meltwater always seeking the lowest point.

Abandoned as the rolling Mid-West hills
Corn-covered, treeless, homeless, yellow sea
Navigable only by auto-guided machines.

Lonely as a bustling city street
Crowded with unknown strangers neighbour-grouped
Excluding those with no known purpose here.

Empty as my mind and heart in your absence
Irreplaceable you.

VISITATION

The brightness in the corner opened my eyes and grew
Into a seagull, no, became an angel
As it stretched upward into my sight,
My consciousness, and spread its wings
As if to embrace me. From beneath them
It stretched out its arms and hands
Holding a plug and flex and screwdriver, and said,
"Heaven's WIFI isn't working, suddenly it failed.
We tried everything, switched it off and on
Frequently, to no effect. But you're an expert,
So our records say. What would you suggest?"
"Hey, wait a minute," I responded, "let us just step back.
You have committed two sins – interrupting
My meditation, and maintaining my personal details
Without my permission." Its brightness dimmed.
It bent its head in shame, and said, "Forgive!"
"But does that work both ways?" I asked. It gulped.
"That's not my job. I cannot guarantee ..."
"Well, can we trade? Exchange two of my sins
For two of yours?" "No," it protested, "that I dare not do,"
And dimmed some more, declined in size and shape.

"I must say Heaven begins to sound like Earth," I said,
"Just brighter when its people are in charge,
And much the same when not." Its glow had now
Diminished. It was barely a foot tall.
I closed my eyes, returned to inner peace
And when I'd finished, it had gone away.

THE CRACK IN THE WINDOW GLASS

The cracked glass was a great gift.
A tiny gap let in the silver light
Which the Edwardian leaves and flowers obscured
And the modesty frosted glass elsewhere precluded.
Where is the crack, or which is it,
That will let into my soul some heat,
Some light, that feeling of fulfilment
For which I have been searching
And every time, against my will, repairing
The crack which I so needed to escape.

WORDS

My hands
Do not make things
Or repair what's broken
But record my enquiring thoughts
On paper

Do others
Care what I think?
Will someone learn my words
To recite them to a lover
One night?

MY HEART

My heart is a dusty box, unopened
For years and years and years.
Its lid has sharp edges, blood-spattered
Where clumsy fingers cut themselves
On my inability to respond as they had hoped.
Inside, in stagnant liquid, flies drown
Having ventured in, unable to escape.
The rags of someone else's clothes
Lie in one corner, people I wished I'd been
But hadn't the courage. One day
I'll throw my heart open to someone
Who'll welcome me in all my silliness,
Break down my stiff defences, capture me,
Absorb me into yet another life.

INTERLUDE

Pause in the music
Instruments laid aside now
Retuning my life

UNIQUE MOMENTS

Rare is each moment, unique its effect on you.
Who do you need, to sit with you in silence
Or to chatter on regarding nothing special,
Skimming the surface of your empty mind
Until, like an angler's hook, some thought inserts
Itself and pulls you to a landing place
For which you had always searched, but never found.
Can you describe it? Has it been seen before?
Been there, if only in a passing dream?
Are you calm? Breathe deeply. Close your eyes.
What happens to you when you loose the ties
Of duty, and let yourself relax for once?

Sit still, forget. No task or duty here.
Breathe in and out. Slowly.
More slowly than before.
Let your hands go, your fingers just for now
Hold nothing, not even a jacket-fold.
Let the cat on your knee go on sleeping.
She knows how to do this.
Like her, close your eyes.
Purr, if you can, deep down.
Begin to drift. What comes?
It will be different every single time.

INDEX OF TITLES

INDEX OF FIRST LINES

THE AUTHOR

Robert was a member of the University of Cambridge Spitzbergen Expedition, 1965, and undertook research in Libya in 1966-67. After graduation, he lectured in environmental sciences in the Universities of London and Exeter, before joining the UK Civil Service. He later spent 7 years as a management consultant, working with central and local government organisations in the UK, Bulgaria and Hungary, and with major manufacturing companies in Belgium, Germany and the USA.

He began writing again after retiring, and has published three poetry collections, "Late Starter" in 2018, "Start to Finish" in 2022 and "Love and Other Thoughts" in 2023. He has won prizes and commendations in the Solihull Writers' Workshop annual poetry and fiction competitions and has published in the quarterly anthologies of the Moseley-based Cannon Poets group. 11 of his short stories are online at www.cafelit.co.uk and his novel "A Magic Flight" was published in 2022.

Always concerned for justice, and now very actively wheelchair-bound, he takes a particular interest in championing the practical interests and difficulties of the aging and the disabled.

Robert Ferguson

Start to
Finish

ISBN 978-3-99131-754-8
74 pages

Wander through your life; the seasons, months, weather,
national events, and personal pleasures. Sit with these poems,
remember, and enjoy.

Robert Ferguson

Love and Other Thoughts

ISBN 978-3-99131-907-8
78 pages

Love comes at every stage in life, and always surprises us, not always happily, but always with a lasting bite.